CW01430498

Quiet Spaces

The brf prayer and spirituality journal

Walk

Edited by Heather Fenton

Published by
The Bible Reading Fellowship
15 The Chambers
Abingdon, OX14 3FE
United Kingdom
Tel: +44 (0)1865 319700
Email: enquiries@brf.org.uk
Website: www.brf.org.uk
BRF is a Registered Charity

ISBN 978 1 84101 872 0
First published 2012
10 9 8 7 6 5 4 3 2 1 0

Acknowledgements
Scripture quotations taken from The Holy Bible, New International Version, copyright © 1973, 1978, 1984 by International Bible Society, are used by permission of Hodder & Stoughton, a member of the Hachette Livre UK Group. All rights reserved. 'NIV' is a registered trademark of International Bible Society. UK trademark number 1448790.

Scripture quotations taken from The New Revised Standard Version of the Bible, Anglicised Edition, copyright © 1989, 1995 by the Division of Christian Education of the National Council of the Churches of Christ in the USA, and are used by permission. All rights reserved.

The editor of *Quiet Spaces* gratefully acknowledges the Ann Griffiths website as the source of the words for the hymns on page 64 and H.A. Hodges as the translator. Details can be found at www.anngriffiths.cardiff.ac.uk and the material is copyright © Cardiff University. The material is used with their permission.

A catalogue record for this book is available from the British Library

Printed in the UK by Rainbow Print

VOLUME 22
Contents

Walk

The Editor writes...

Heather Fenton is the Editor of *Quiet Spaces*.

Driving back from a funeral just now, I saw a small child balancing along the top of a wall and apparently enjoying every moment of it. She was so small, it would not have been long ago that people were saying of her, 'Is she walking yet?' These new skills, which parents long to see, are soon taken for granted and become the subject of experimentation, sometimes accompanied by frustration, for enjoyment or out of necessity. Like for the lady whose funeral I had been attending, growing older may mean the loss of this basic skill with accompanying frustrations. Yes, walking is important!

So in this issue of *Quiet Spaces* we explore the idea of walking. I explore walking through the eye of the Psalmist and, having an interest in pilgrimage, I have included a brief article about the history of pilgrimage and information about some walking pilgrimage routes. Margaret Harvey starts her column by adding three more ways of walking to the list I have, in her article 'Thinking about ways of walking'. Each of them has something to tell us about our walk with God, and together they could form an outline for a Quiet Day. Carol Jerman walks with some very unusual and interesting travelling companions while Tony Horsfall tells us more about Watchman Nee, a very brave man. When the Communist Party began to gain power in China in 1949, Watchman Nee learnt to stand his ground against those who wanted to eliminate Christianity.

David Spriggs from Bible Society writes about Psalm 23. There seems to be only one direct reference to walking—'through the valley of the shadows' (v. 4, NIV)—but a closer look reveals that the image of walking is present everywhere. Holly Price points out that our journey through life is not a mission to earn the right, eventually, to rest with God—rather our starting point is rest, and we walk to live out, work out and enjoy the rest Christ has given us. Mark Berry is fascinated by St Brendan the Navigator and St Columba, and he tells us how these saints encourage him and those around him to 'walk with God in God's world'. Liz Pacey has written some prayers again this time. She imagines walking in various situations and gives us prayers which fit these, including walking to work or school, around the supermarket, walking alone and also with a dog, and a prayer for those who cannot walk at all.

So take a quiet stroll through all the good things just waiting for you to stroll past, to stop and inspect, and then go on refreshed in your walk with God. And if you would like to send comments or ideas about *Quiet Spaces*, there is now an email address for this purpose, so all you have to do is walk to your computer and email us on quietspaces@brf.org.uk or you can write to us at the address on the subscription page at the back (page 80). It would be good to hear from you! Also, you may like to think about taking out a *Quiet Spaces* subscription for a friend, or passing on your copy when you have finished using it.

Walk for life— Psalm 23

author

The Revd Dr David Spriggs is a Baptist minister, currently working as Head of Church Relations for Bible Society, where he has also been Project Director for The Open Book. He has written a number of books.

Walking and Psalm 23

'Do you fancy a walk?' I wonder how often we say or hear those words. They are an invitation to spend leisure time on light exercise so that we can enjoy the scenery, listen to the birds and, maybe, the sound of a stream or the waves crashing on rocks. Afterwards, we'll have a relaxing drink in a pub, perhaps before returning home for a good night's sleep. Such walking is pleasant and relaxing. There are many other kinds of walks, for example, for health's sake—to lose weight or because of a heart problem. Then there are charity walks, while for some there is no choice but a toilsome walk of many miles to collect water from a stream or spring. So what kind of walking is envisaged in this psalm? It is certainly a 'walk for life'.

Walking is a very human activity. Unless we have a physical disability that makes it impossible or inappropriate, walking is an activity available to us all. Only some can sprint or climb

Consider the following:

The Lord will establish you...
if you keep the commandments...
and walk in his ways.
DEUTERONOMY 28:9, NRSV

... your servants who walk before you
with all their heart.
2 CHRONICLES 6:14

Those who walk blamelessly and do
what is right.
PSALM 15:2

Just as Christ was raised from the
dead..., so we too might walk in
newness of life.
ROMANS 6:4

The NRSV translation has 'hidden' many of the references to 'walk', where it means consistent behaviour or way of life. To gain some sense of the frequency of this idiom, please refer to a good concordance which is based on the King James Version of the Bible.

Another reason why 'walking' is prevalent in the Bible is that it involves action. Being a Christian may be about believing, certainly involving our inner thoughts and emotions, and it is also about belonging—relationships and community are vital components of our Christian living, but sharing cups of

mountains, only a few have the courage to bungee jump, but most of us can walk, for example to the shops. Not all can afford to sail a yacht or drive a sports car, but walking is open to almost everyone. Perhaps that is one reason why it is a favourite biblical metaphor for living life with God—it is not elitist, sexist or ageist, it is what unites us all on our 'pilgrim way'!

tea and cake is not the sum total of it. Walking reminds us that our Christian life involves doing things and going somewhere too—it includes becoming.

Walking is also something that requires persistence. I envy those who can run 100 metres in less than ten seconds but walking takes much longer. Of course, sprinting demands endless training, but what we see and remember are the few seconds of glory. Walking is essentially about keeping on keeping on, one foot in front of another for as long as it takes, whatever the weather!

You may be wondering why we focus on 'walking' in Psalm 23. There seems to be only one direct reference to walking: 'through the darkest valley' (v. 4). A closer look, however, reveals that the image of walking is present everywhere. It is similar in life—we do a lot of walking that isn't exactly 'a walk': getting up from the chair to make a cup of tea, going to the door to let someone in, climbing the stairs to go to bed. It's only when we break a leg that we realise just how much walking we do in a day! This psalm is about living ordinary lives but in the companionship of God. The walk of the sheep envisaged here was often much the same each day. Sometimes, when conditions demanded it, the walk would take a radically different route, as drought required new grass and water to be found.

Pause for a moment and ask yourself whether the walk of your life is the normal one—the regular rhythm and routine—or whether, for whatever reason, it is a walk that involves change—pleasant change, such as holidays, or disturbing change, like a bereavement or illness.

All of these aspects of walking and more are included in Psalm 23. What is the 'more'? It is the dynamic of the partnership. Frequently, walking implies some kind of equality, of sharing and of agreement as to when and where we'll walk, how long we'll pause or sit, when we'll turn for home.

This psalm is not a psalm about equals! Make no mistake—there is a shepherd and we are the sheep. In a culture like ours, where all authority is questioned and individual freedom and 'rights' deeply shape our psyche, this is an aspect of the psalm with which we probably need to wrestle. It doesn't fit easily with the way we live our lives. Yet, we do need to get the tone of this right, otherwise we cannot share the heart of this journey. Even though the shepherd is clearly in charge, there is no sense here of authoritarianism, of bullying, of coercion, of unreasonable demand or cruelty. 'The Lord is my Shepherd' is not a frightened cry from the oppressed; it is a joyful testimony to privilege and promise, security and hope. So as we prepare to set out on our walk through this psalm, do take some time to ask yourself how you see and relate to this shepherd. Is it as this sheep to this shepherd? If not, ask God to draw you into the fullness of this kind of relationship.

Maybe it would be helpful to review what experiences might hinder us being as comfortable with the shepherd as this palmist is. There could be issues to clear out of the way. Spending time thanking God for his protective love and providential leading may help to take us further into the truth of this picture.

Walking through Psalm 23

Verse 2

This is a good place to start: resting and refreshing, plenty of attractive food and water and no threat here, as the pools are quiet. Sometimes water can be a raging torrent or polluted, but not here—just what we need and long for. This beautiful picture assures us of God's fundamental generosity towards us and of his desire for our lives. It is so important that we have a healthy understanding of the shepherd's care for us and pleasure in us; he is full of kindness and goodwill. Any image we have of a malevolent or capricious deity is wrong. We need to fill our minds as well as our hearts with this truth. We may even need to seek for the Holy Spirit's help to purge our memory banks. If that is the case for you, then it would be good to return to this verse and stay with it frequently; spend time resting, imagine that you are drinking from the clear pools and are being refreshed by all the blessings that God pours into your life. Come and enter this picture many times a day, indeed whenever you find yourself wondering what God is really like, or when the suspicion creeps into your minds that he may not, after all, love you deeply and passionately.

The fact remains that, in order to get to this restoring place, we need to have walked with the shepherd. This lush grass is not where we usually live, as most of us are not normally surrounded by English pastureland. So as we begin today, perhaps we can listen to God's call and, no matter whether we are feeling optimistic or anxious or depressed, we can decide that we will let him lead our lives and keep going with him. If we are enjoying God's good provision, then we can be glad, thanking him for his goodness. He gives us new strength.

Verse 3

We cannot expect to spend all of our lives in such a wonderful and restorative place. There was more to life for the sheep than this and there is more to our lives. God provided the sabbath day (Exodus 20:8–11), but this was in the context of working on the other six! The new strength God provides is there so that we can move on. If we sit all our lives fattening ourselves on lush grass, our legs will become useless.

Where does the shepherd plan to take us? Does he have a plan? There will be difficulties along the way, so in addition to the resources we need to gather for the day's journey, we also need the confidence that the shepherd knows where he is taking us: 'He leads [us] in right paths' (Psalm 23:3). What exactly 'paths of righteousness' might entail is a source of much stimulation for biblical scholars. Are they right moral directions; are they pathways of vindication before our accusers; are they safe and clear routes; are they equivalent to blessing

and salvation? Whatever view we take, we can be sure of three things: first, they are paths that are known to the shepherd as he has been this way before; then, it is not unknown territory with problems he has no knowledge about; as we go this way today, he is just ahead of us. He doesn't provide a map and say, 'On you go then, find your own way.' Finally, they are tracks that take us somewhere (they are not aimless; the journey is not simply filling in time as when walking up and down at an airport) and the outcome will be beneficial.

Consider which of these three aspects of 'right paths' is most important for you to be assured about today.

'I walk through the deepest valley' (v. 4). Around the beginning of 2011, this is how it seemed to me. Two of my children's marriages were shattering, one involving three grandchildren; the wife of our third child was taken into hospital with a life-threatening illness. This all hit us within a few weeks. I felt that I couldn't 'press on toward the goal…' (Philippians 3:14), I couldn't even walk. All I could do was to limp along as the pain was so great and the weight of perplexity and anxiety so heavy. As I attempted to imagine the future, the shadows were truly horrific— 'what if…?' I was approaching paralysis!

But this Psalm doesn't say that we will not go through difficult times. It says, 'Even if…' or maybe 'Even when…', for such times will come to us on our walk with God. These words reshape the meaning and the experience.

How can we cope when the times are really tough? Perhaps the key is more in the word 'Lord' than in the words, 'I fear no evil'. This could be an attempt to stir ourselves, to tell ourselves to be more courageous, to shake off the self-pity. Sometimes that can help, but it can lead to collapse as well! But we do not walk alone. Please note how the poetry conveys the message. The first three verses have referred to God in the

> *Then remember the words 'as he has promised'. Thank God for his promise to you, that your life today is covered by his promise.*

Verse 4

Now the darkness closes in; the threats seem to mount up and become more menacing. Life is threatened and there seems no comfort or practical solution. Financial difficulties escalate with credit card debts, reducing income and increasing bills. Relationships have fragmented and the bitterness and recriminations are causing further pain. The prognosis from the medical investigation is serious. Life is very tough for many of us. Yet, the shadows create an even deeper sense of foreboding, generating frightening shapes from which our minds construct monsters. What else might be just hidden from our knowledge? As we are on this downward path from which there seems no escape, we project harsher realities and terrify ourselves even more.

third person singular; now it shifts to the second person: 'He' changes to 'You'. God comes closer in the grammar!

When we are overwhelmed, then the first thing is to utter God's name, 'Lord'. As we do this, often with considerable struggle, we start to refocus. We release the power of our previous experiences, of the truths of scripture, of the promises of God. The cross of Jesus tells us that God is with us in the darkest times, even if we cannot see him at all. We are not alone, even in death, whether the death of a loved one or our own death.

'I will fear no evil; for you are with me' (v. 4). Even when we cannot sense his presence, he is still at work guiding and guarding.

'Your rod and your staff—they comfort me' (v. 4). He is the shepherd, committed to laying down his life for the sheep.

Often calling (perhaps 'whispering' would be more accurate) 'Lord' was all I could manage. The daughter-in-law has survived and narrowly avoided an invasive operation; she is now on the way to recovery. The two marriages are still in a broken state. They haven't improved, so we still carry great sorrow. But God is guiding us with his rod and staff. Even limping along is walking with God and he sticks with us!

Where are you now on your journey? Are you in restful pastures? Are you immersed in terrifying darkness? Do you sense you are moving towards one of those harrowing times? Are you emerging from one? Recall, 'Lord, you are my shepherd'.

Remember friends or family who are in such dark times. Pray for them that they may discover God's caring presence and love for them.

After the walk

So, to the journey's end. No matter how long and challenging, or how pleasant and rewarding, each walk will come to its proper conclusion. This is ours.

You prepare a table before me in the presence of my enemies; you anoint my head with oil; my cup overflows. Surely goodness and mercy shall follow me all the days of my life.
PSALM 23:5—6

As Paul might have said, 'Hope will not disappoint us' (Romans 5:5). In the same way we may keep looking at the holiday brochure when we have months still to wait, so we can keep returning to and resting in this powerful image, each step of our walk with God.

CAROL JERMAN

Travelling companions

I have some unusual travelling companions. Their names are Eddie and Kubera, and they are fully trained trekking llamas, which accompany me as I lead people on walks in the beautiful countryside of our part of the Berwyn Mountains.

I like to walk alone, but walking with the llamas and my customers is quite a different thing from that. Walking alone is to me most delightful, for I am entranced by the beauty, absorbed by the interest of the natural world, and I praise God in pure wonder. When I trek with the llamas, there is a sharing of the joy, but also the responsibility of looking out for the needs of my companions, both human and animal, at all times. When I was young in faith, I understood my walk with God to be my individual

author

Carol Jerman is a retired teacher and a Reader in the Church in Wales. She takes people walking in the Berwyn Mountains, accompanied by her llamas.

journey with him. Now I can see that in fact I am walking in the company of others, and the focus of my actions and my communications with God must be largely concerned with the needs of my companions.

There is no separation between spiritual and natural. Heaven and earth are filled with his glory. If we crave to be more like Jesus, then the lessons our souls learn in every situation impact upon our faith and our understanding of the ways of God with us. I find that I often learn spiritual lessons best by perceiving the principles that are at work in everyday situations. When I first bought my llamas and began training them, I had no idea of how much they would teach me.

My first lesson was in patience and persistence, for my llamas were not quickly persuaded to cooperate. They

... fully trained trekking llamas

I had no idea of how much the llamas would teach me

© Carol Jerman

> I am entranced by the beauty, absorbed by the interest of the natural world

are large animals with minds of their own and I have generally found that they like to make a protest first, before complying with what I want. These days, this often consists in their not coming when they are called. They have about five acres of steep pasture in which to roam and often choose to stay at the top. They know very well what they are being asked to do but will wait until I have climbed the hill to the very top before they gallop down, fleet as deer on the rough ground, to wait at the bottom for me to arrive and put on their halters. It is as if they are saying, 'Yes, we will work with you, but only because we want to, not because we have to.' This is just a small remnant of their behaviour during training! They will also 'go on strike' during a trek at times: if they think they have not had a fair break in which to graze, they will simply lie down and refuse to move. It's no use getting frustrated or annoyed. Only

quiet persistence, backed by lack of pride, will succeed. My plans and my timing must have in them the space for irregularities in the llamas' behaviour. The reward for giving them the space to be animals and not machines is an increasing bond of loyalty, their increasing wish to please me and to take their lead from me. How much more, when working with other human beings, our equals, must we give one another space to decide what to do! It is all too easy to become frustrated by our brothers and sisters in Christ when their actions, or lack of actions, delay or spoil our plans. It is all too tempting to be dismayed by lack of quick agreement.

Training the llamas took a long time, not because of their nature, but because of my lack of understanding. Eventually, the lesson began to penetrate. I had to observe them and learn to understand them. They were supremely observant and would pick up any sense of frustration I had and react badly to it. Instead of being preoccupied with my own difficulties, I had to observe the llamas and work with what they gave me. I had to reflect on each success and failure. These were lessons in greater quietness and humility of soul—definitely transferrable skills. Animals, which are without human language, can teach us a great deal, if we have the humility to respect them enough to learn from them. I began to realise anew how often human words can be a smoke-screen. Far too often I have taken what people say at face value instead of discerning what is really going on. I knew these things before, but working with the llamas every day, trying to make progress with their training, effected in me new habits of mind and action. I discovered more fully the value of reflective observation and the futility of my own energies and assertiveness.

Once the treks began, I understood how important these lessons had been. Only by being continually observant can I conduct a successful trek. And what is true on a trek applies to our shared journey in the church. We have to look out for one another. I am my brother's keeper, and he is mine.

On a trek, I am the leader. This means that I am responsible for the safety and the comfort of all the others, both humans and animals. My plans and my timing have to have enough space in them to accommodate varied needs and choices. I am often surprised by how people react and by what they

> The lessons our souls learn in every situation impact upon our faith

can or cannot do, but I must not show surprise. I have to be entirely alert but also entirely relaxed. I need to notice that Kubera's lower lip is quivering slightly and realise that the shrill, excitable voice of the child leading him is making him anxious. I need to notice that Eddie is pawing at a dusty patch under a bank where the sheep have been lying and encourage his handler to lead him on before he rolls in the dust, damaging his pack saddle and squashing our picnic. The front llama won't go on. I have to understand that he's tired of leading and wants the other llama to take his turn at the front. I have to understand that what is normal walking for me, over rough, wet grass, avoiding thistles and cow pats, isn't normal for everyone. I have to be ready to make conversation or not, for some people want to be friendly, while others want their own space. I have to be able to pick up each person's level of confidence and match them with a suitable llama. I have to do all these things and many more in a way that never makes anyone feel silly. It is never about what I am getting out of a trek. It is all about observing the others in order to promote their success. This has been like a parable to me about how to behave in the church.

Llamas can like or dislike their handlers. They like clear signals and calm behaviour. People can do all sorts of things to make a llama anxious. On one occasion, a man asked me why his llama seemed to be afraid of him. I told him that his hand movements were too fast. 'Oh,' he said. 'In London, we have to do everything at top speed.' 'Not here,' I replied. 'Here, you have to do everything at llama pace.' Shortly after this, I watched the tension roll off him and his family as he slowed down and moved in silence up the slope into the expanding view of hills and sky.

The steady accumulation of such experiences has worked in me an increased realism about my own

> The focus of my actions and my communications with God must be largely concerned with the needs of my companions

spiritual journey. It is, in truth, not *my* journey but *our* journey. I am not a solitary pilgrim but a part of church. My spirituality must equip me to understand and to serve. I must be aware of the walking of others and be ready to promote their success. I must always be alert, observant, hearing beyond the words and never be preoccupied either by my own enjoyment or by my own needs. This is demanding, and sometimes I crave to walk alone. It would be so simple, just God and me walking together through life! But this is not the reality. I can best love him by expressing his love to others.

The things we learn are usually the things we already know—or at least, we think we know them, only to find we have to learn them again at a new level. I am amazed at how much my unusual travelling companions have taught me. Working with them has changed me as a person, altered my approach to church life, brought about greater stillness. Trekking with them has necessitated greater release from myself, greater awareness of others. The whole experience, over these last six years, has altered my concept of spirituality. God has taught and blessed me in ways I had never expected, so I thank him for my llamas.

HOLLY PRICE

The path lit by Christ

The gods may not have given Sisyphus the most glamorous role, nor the most stretching, but he is happy with his lot in life. His task: to roll a rock up a hill again and again and again. Naturally he does have his moments. There are times when he longs for a smoother rock or a smaller hill. But then, he reminds him-self, both could have been worse. Most of the time he feels lucky. The gods do not compel him to take a certain route, so he is left with the choice of an infinite number of possible paths. As he searches for the perfect path, he secretly hopes that it will always elude him. If he slips (accidentally or other-wise), he can meander back down the hill, avoiding their disapproving looks.

This is how the author Michael Foley envisions this character from Greek mythology. He infers that Sisyphus is content in his task—but, according to the legend, the punishment leaves him eternally frustrated.

Life can sometimes feel like this—an endless cycle of arbitrary tasks. We strive, strive, strive, but we don't seem to advance. What is our time on earth all about?

'To survive is to strive.' This is the conclusion of Foley's book, *The Age*

author

Holly Price is a film fanatic and works as a writer and editor for the Damaris Trust.

expects to pay its own way, the most crucial revelation is that everything worthwhile is a gift from God.

Getting out of the blocks

Sit, Walk, Stand. These three words, which make up the title of a compilation of sermons spoken by Watchman Nee, are ordered very deliberately. Nee explains Christ's countercultural approach to life:

Most Christians make the mistake of trying to walk in order to be able to sit, but that is a reversal of the true order. Our natural reason says, If we do not walk, how can we ever reach the goal? What can we attain without effort? But Christianity is a queer business! If we seek to attain something, we miss everything. For Christianity begins not with a big DO, but with a big DONE.
Watchman Nee, *Sit, Walk, Stand*, p.2

of Absurdity: Why Modern Life Makes it Hard to be Happy. 'For the age that expects everything to be easy,' he writes, 'the most crucial revelation is that everything worthwhile is difficult' (Michael Foley, *The Age of Absurdity*, Simon & Schuster, 2010, pp. 68–69).

Christ preached a very different path. He too confronted the futility of humanity's endeavours, but he provided a solution. Perhaps, for the age that

We do not need to gain ground in God's affection. God has already 'raised us up with Christ and seated us with him in

... an endless cycle of arbitrary tasks

the heavenly realms' (Ephesians 2:6, NIV). We have attained the highest position. We have reached the greatest goal. And we got there by grace.

Our journey through life is not a mission to earn the right, eventually, to rest with God. Rather, our starting point is rest, and we walk to live out, work out and enjoy the rest Christ has given us. As God told the spiritually meandering Israelites, his people advance by relying on him:

In repentance and rest is your salvation, in quietness and trust is your strength.
ISAIAH 30:15

In the Christian life, it is pointless to get up and running before resting in Christ.

Life as it's meant to be

So what compels us to walk at all? Why must we face the daily grind of countering the grain? We trust Christ for our salvation and our heavenly destination, but what inspires us to follow him now? 'The Cave', a song by Brit Award-winning folk band Mumford

> Our starting point is rest

> Everything worthwhile is a gift from God

& Sons, contains a line that might help us. It explains that the more you become convinced that your maker is dependable, the more you want to depend upon him.

The more we walk with God— aligning ourselves with his thoughts and ways—the more we appreciate all that he has given to us. The persona in 'The Cave' cries for freedom and truth that will restore his life to its intended pattern. As John tells us, Christ is himself the way, the truth and the life, and holding to his teaching sets us free (John 14:6; 8:31). No other track leads to true life.

What is the point of being seated with Christ in the heavenly realms, if in the earthly realms we do not feel the benefit of his life and freedom, or bear the stamp of his way and truth?

Christ beckons us to follow his lead with his help:

Come to me, all you who are weary and burdened, and I will give you rest. Take my yoke upon you and learn from me, for I am gentle and humble in heart, and you will find rest for your souls. For my yoke is easy and my burden is light.

MATTHEW 11:28–30

Why must we face the daily grind of countering the grain?

Christ has removed the yoke of sin, which weighed us down with the shame of guilt and the fear of death. He has given us a new yoke, one that is made to fit us perfectly. And he has yoked us with himself that we might walk the straight path together. Just as a weak new ox ploughs alongside a large experienced one, so we walk with Christ, learning from him and letting him bear the load.

Tracking heavenly footprints

Like the furrows oxen plough, the path Christians walk is a straightforward one. 'What does the Lord require of you?' says Micah. 'To act justly and to love mercy and to walk humbly with your God' (Micah 6:8). Of course, we have more than instructions to go by; we have a living guide.

Let's stand in Christ's shoes and walk around in them for a moment. He took an uncharted path. His feet were beautiful in the biblical sense, as they spread the news of God's kingdom with

urgency and authority. Along the way he stopped, knelt down and reached out to heal people from physical, emotional and spiritual ailments, even from death. He trod on the turbulent waves of the sea. He washed the feet of his betrayer.

He was down to earth, but he was also otherworldly, even possessing the power to forgive sins. Ultimately, his feet bore him to the cross under the weight of the sins of the world. They still bear the scars of that day, when he chose justice tempered with mercy in accordance with God's wishes.

How much does your life weigh?

'If anyone would come after me,' Christ said, 'he must deny himself and take up his cross daily and follow me' (Mark 8:34). Our standard is not the law; our standard is Christ's sacrifice. Watchman Nee suggests that our relationships are the battleground where this principle stands or falls.

Up in the Air is a film about relating to people in an era of brutal job cuts and online communities. George Clooney's character, Ryan Bingham, has formed a philosophy that enables him to travel light in life. He sees relationships as unnecessary baggage and strives to empty his life of anything that might slow him down. His mantra is: moving is living.

Christ's answer to this is stark: moving is sacrifice. 'Whoever wants to save his life will lose it, but whoever loses his life for me and for the gospel will save it' (Mark 8:35). As Christians, we ought to 'carry each other's burdens', 'honour one another above [our]selves' and 'lay down our lives for our brothers' (Galatians 6:2; Romans 12:10; 1 John 3:16). More than that, we should 'loose the chains of injustice and untie the cords of the yoke, to set the oppressed free' (Isaiah 58:6). Basically, we 'must walk as Jesus did' (1 John 2:6).

Suddenly the load feels heavier than ever! Perhaps a better question than, 'How heavy is my life?' is, 'Who is holding my life together?'

What is our time on earth all about?

The cross of Christ is our model. But we are living not under the law but under the grace that came to us because Christ resolutely trudged up to Calvary. The standard has once and for all been met.

The difference between staggering and striding

I once read the story of a man who crossed the Mississippi on foot when it was frozen. Half way across he lost his confidence and began to panic. He finished his crossing on his stomach, soaked and chilled. Imagine his face when, almost immediately after standing on the shore, he saw another man, sitting on a large sleigh loaded with pig iron, wave cheerily as he passed and drive over in complete safety.

Now it will be like that for some Christians travelling through from earth to heaven supported 'only' on the promises of God. Some will go through their whole pilgrimage worried, fretting, hardly daring to believe their God and Saviour can cope with their failures and doubts and fears and will keep them to the end. Others press on with confidence and even joy, sometimes slipping but regaining their foothold and pressing on, confident in God, determined to serve and love and obey him and praising him as if in prospect of glory.

'Which are you?' asks Peter Lewis in his book on Hebrews 11. 'Do you act as if you are on thin ice or solid rock?' (Peter Lewis, *God's Honours List*, Hodder and Stoughton, 1996) The following chapter of Hebrews urges us to race towards heaven, confident in Christ who is both the 'author and perfecter of our faith'.

According to another Peter, Christ has not just set the standard; he has supplied everything we need to reach it:

His divine power has given us everything we need for life and godliness through our knowledge of him who called us by his own glory and goodness. Through these he has given us his very great and precious promises, so that through them you may participate in the divine nature and escape the corruption in the world caused by evil desires.

2 PETER 1:3–4

What are these promises that we can stride out upon?

The Sovereign Lord is my strength; he makes my feet like the feet of a deer, he enables me to go on the heights.

HABAKKUK 3:19

The Lord is the everlasting God, the Creator of the ends of the earth. He will not grow tired or weary... Those who hope in the Lord will renew their strength. They will soar on wings like eagles; they will run and not grow weary, they will walk and not be faint.

ISAIAH 40:28, 31

I will walk among you and be your God, and you will be my people. I am the Lord your God, who brought you out of Egypt so that you would no longer be slaves to the Egyptians; I broke the bars of your yoke and enabled you to walk with heads held high.

LEVITICUS 26:12–13

Come to me, all you who are weary and burdened, and I will give you rest. Take my yoke upon you and learn from me, for I am gentle and humble in heart, and you will find rest for your souls. For my yoke is easy and my burden is light.

MATTHEW 11:28–30

These are just a few to meditate upon. You might like to start your own list—a reminder to walk the trail Christ blazed for us.

Prodigal paths

I'm independent
Freethinking
A pioneer of my own path, walked at my
own pace

Faith is to hurl oneself—in the dark—into
the arms of a person
who holds all the answers but won't
show you his cards

That's too much risk
Who accepts terms like
'Deny yourself, take up your cross and
follow me'?

My walk may be ungainly at times,
clumsy even
But I'm working on it
And it's fun

I see you—tracking my regrets, charting
my failures, imagining my
Emptiness
But you can't see me
I
am my own, and
I
go where
I
like

*I wake up every day and see that it
holds no meaning, nothing has a limit,
no one's ever wrong and truth is just a
myth we search for sometimes*

*I entertain every indulgence, enjoying
life's pleasures
… but in a moment of quiet
I find that they have led me in circles
around myself*

*Instead of being filled with happiness
and freedom
I feel chained and addicted
Or else a dozen things call for me at
once, distracting me into dizziness and
keeping my eyes from focusing beyond
at someone worth staring at*

*The truth is, I'm so broken I can't pick
up the pieces
And so busy running nowhere, I'm lost
and turning back holds no hope
I long to belong to someone and some
purpose
I long to see my God, take his hand and
for us to adventure together*

*But when he picks up my heart and
makes it whole again
I have to promise it to him
not
bit
by
bit
Whole*

*I'd have to take down my defences and
left vulnerable
admit my route is wrong
I'd have to
reveal the real me—a child—
And to commit to race every day for just
one desire*

© HOLLY PRICE 2011

MARK BERRY

Holy wandering

Something is changing; the wind has turned; the horizon has shifted. One of the responses to a changing world, where feelings of insecurity are rising, where certainty feels like an illusion, is to retreat into a circle of protection where we see the world outside as a threat to our existence, as the enemy. The other response is to relish the challenge, to become adventurers, exiles, vagabonds and pilgrims!

In the midst of a changing world many years ago St Columba wrote:

author

Mark Berry is a Lay Pioneer Minister and Mission Partner with CMS, who, in 2005, after years exploring community with and for young people, founded a community called safespace in Telford, Shropshire.

God counselled Abraham to leave his own country and go in pilgrimage into the land, which God has shown him, to wit, the 'Land of Promise'... Now the good counsel which God enjoined here on the father of the faithful is incumbent on all the faithful; that is to leave their country and their land, their wealth and their worldly delight for the sake of the lord of elements, and go in perfect pilgrimage in imitation of him.

CHADWICK, NORA, *THE AGE OF THE SAINTS IN THE EARLY CELTIC CHURCH*, OXFORD UNIVERSITY PRESS, 1961, P. 83

This is not pilgrimage as a trip to a holy place; this is not the pilgrimage of destination but the pilgrimage of living. Often now we find the word 'pilgrim' being replaced by 'peregrinate', defined by the Oxford English Dictionary as one who 'wanders around from place to place'—in the context of faith, holy wanderers. Perhaps the most famous historic peregrinate is the Irish Abbot St Brendan. Brendan established several monastic communities, but it is for his journey that he is most renowned and for which he has attracted the epithet 'the Navigator'. The great saga, the *Navigatio Sancti Brendani Abbatis*, tells of his seven-year journey from the Dingle Peninsula in south-west Ireland to what is thought to be America. The story tells how Brendan climbed the mountain near his family home in Dingle to seek God's call.

How do we allow a pilgrim spirit to shape the way we view our relationship with God and our relationship with others?

> Brendan established several monastic communities, but it is for his journey that he is most renowned

After spending time looking over the sea from the top of what is now known as Mount Brandon, he built a small leather fishing boat. He then set sail on to the unknown ocean on what would become a seven-year journey across the northern ocean. As they sailed, he encouraged his brothers, saying,

Fear not, brothers, for our God will be unto us a helper, a mariner, and a pilot; take in the oars and helm, keep the sails set, and may God do unto us, His servants and His little vessel, as He willeth.

NAVIGATIO SANCTI BRENDANI ABBATIS, EDITION BY P. F. MORAN, TRANSLATED BY DENIS O'DONOGHUE, PUBLISHED BY D. O'DONOGHUE, DATE OF TRANSLATION 1893

There are two key aspects to this part of the tale to which I want to draw attention. The first is the simple preparation. Brendan begins by taking time to meditate on what he believes God to be calling him to do. He has heard tell of a far-off land but before throwing himself into the journey, he stops, takes time and wrestles with God's call for him. After that he simply goes to the harbour and builds his boat, a currach. The currach is still used today for fishing the creeks and inlets of south-west Ireland and for racing.

It is not an ocean-going ship. Brendan and his monks used local tools, local knowledge and local wisdom in a spirit of prayer and meditation to prepare for their unknown journey.

The second aspect of the story is perhaps the most challenging. It is simply Brendan's willingness to go into the wild unknown. I have stood at the point from which Brendan set sail and, believe me, sailing from there is not a comfortable thought. The waves crash and thunder in small caves along the cliffs and the wind is funnelled into the natural creek. The landscape itself, its sights, sounds and smells, all point

without question to the power of what lies beyond.

Brendan is said to have knelt in the sand before leaving and prayed this prayer.

Shall I abandon, O King of mysteries,
The soft comforts of home?
Shall I leave the prints of my knees on
the sandy beach,
A record of my final prayer in my native
land?
Shall I then suffer every kind of wound,
That the sea can inflict?
Shall I take my tiny boat across the wide
sparkling ocean?
O King of the Glorious Heaven,
Shall I go of my own choice upon the sea?
O Christ, will You help me on the wild
waves?

(PRAYER ATTRIBUTED TO ST BRENDAN BEFORE SETTING SAIL)

Ann Morisy writes:

Journeying out requires the capacity to rise above the anxiety associated with encountering and embracing a potentially overwhelming, outside world.

I can well imagine that Brendan would have felt this anxiety! Yet, Morisy is not writing about ancient journeys but about mission today. She goes on to say:

My case is that when we journey out, without power, aware of our vulnerability and all the time risking that we may be overwhelmed, we will find ourselves being church and doing holistic mission.

ANN MORISY, *JOURNEYING OUT: A NEW APPROACH TO CHRISTIAN MISSION*, MOREHOUSE PUBLISHING, 2004)

It is not hard to see the parallels emerging for Christians as we seek to walk humbly with God in the world in which we now find ourselves, a world that at times is scary and alien, yet a world in which we are called to live. Living in this world, which seems so strange and uncertain, where in many ways we do not feel at home, challenges us to reflect on our own sense of spirituality, to let go of ideas of power and control, of changing the world to our way, to accepting that we are foreigners.

Sir Francis Drake is said to have prayed:

*May we be disturbed, when
We are too well pleased with ourselves,
When our dreams have come true
Because we have dreamed too little,
When we arrived safely
Because we sailed too close to the shore.*

FRANCIS DRAKE, C.1577

This challenge to be disturbed captures this everyday pilgrim spirituality. We do not pray for individual security but for learning and opportunity. Underpinning the life of the pilgrim is one word: risk! Brendan took a huge risk in setting off on his journey, but it's not simply about the first step—each step means taking risks. We all make big mistakes, we fail regularly, but somehow that has to become a positive part of who we are. To fail means that we have taken risks; to fail means that we are pushing ourselves beyond our comfort zones; to fail means that we allow space for God! As Paulo Coelho wrote in his novel *The Pilgrimage* (HarperCollins, 1999), 'The ship is safest when it is in port, but that's not what ships were built for.'

There are seven stages of pilgrimage, which can form a useful tool for reflection.

1. What does it mean to be a pilgrim?

This is a question of identity, of reflecting each day on who we are. What are our attitudes and values, and how do we reflect them in reality? How do we allow a pilgrim spirit to shape the way we view our relationship with God and our relationship with others?

> To fail means that we have taken risks; to fail means that we are pushing ourselves beyond our comfort zones; to fail means that we allow space for God

2. What are the signs that lead me on the journey?

Any journey has twists and turns and is non-linear. It has moments and episodes that in themselves have value and are important to notice, honour and celebrate—even the difficult ones. What have been the key God moments in our lives, the places where we have encountered God in the ordinary and everyday?

3. Who are my companions and do I really know them?

We need to recognise that this is a community journey, with all the intimacy and vulnerability that goes with it. We are with some people for a short time while others we are able to see grow and change and they have an impact on us over a longer period. We need to ask real questions about how much we know these people. Regardless of time,

This is the calling
on all of us

they are our companions and need to be treated as such, not merely as acquaintances at a common event.

4. What is the story of the people and places?

What are the myths and legends of the place we find ourselves in and its social, spiritual, and political history? What do people believe about their community? What do we really know about the people we meet, their dreams, their sense of spirituality, their struggles and sorrows?

5. Become part of the story

We mustn't simply be an observer, for the minute we step out we are connected to the story, part of it and potentially shapers of it. This is the point when we stop and commit to God's purpose, when we commit to the challenge of Micah 6:8, to walk humbly with God.

6. Become aware of where heaven and earth touch

How do we meet God each day in the ordinary, in ordinary people, ordinary events? How do we train our spiritual eyes through our spiritual practices to recognise God each day?

7. Become aware that we are all the people of God

We are global and local, connected to all people and things in and of God. We have to learn to be both respectful of others and their traditions, and critical of hypocrisy. We know that others have rich treasures and gifts to give. We are all one body, and it is imperative that we are humble enough to allow them to give and allow ourselves to receive.

These seven steps are ongoing. We need to reflect constantly on where we are and on what the current challenges are for us as individuals and as a community. One of the key aspects of a pilgrimage is that it is a journey of episodes. Each moment needs to be learned from and to be allowed to shape our faith. Along with these big questions, it is helpful to develop a simple weekly rhythm which grounds the reality of living a pilgrim spirituality. Here in Telford we use a seven-part tool:

❖ See and appreciate something new in creation
❖ Explore something about Jesus
❖ Listen in silence to the Spirit
❖ Bless and be blessed by someone
❖ Listen to and share a God story with someone
❖ Pray for and ask for prayer from someone
❖ Rest

These simple promises are at the root of what we need to be equipped, resourced and supported in living a life that exudes mission; to reflect a missional and holistic spirituality and to live that life alongside those for whom church has no meaning or real-life connection, and to be focused on being agents of transformation in the world in which we find ourselves.

... to be focused on being agents of transformation in the world in which we find ourselves

To live a pilgrim spirituality means recognising that life is a journey which is lived according to God's purpose and merged in God's purpose, in a rhythm of humble relationship with God and with others, not a dualism of 'spiritual' and 'secular' life (for example, church life and work life). This is the heart of the pilgrim, the inspiration of Brendan, Aidan, Chad and a man called Jesus, who walked the roads of Palestine 2000-odd years ago. This is the calling on all of us to be peacemakers, disciples and children of God in a strange land. This is a faith lived 'on the road', where whatever happens, happens, and where we pray each day, 'May the way be led by your will, God, not mine.'

LIZ PACEY

Walking prayerfully through life

author

Liz Pacey is a Reader in the Church of England, a freelance writer and a mature theology and ministry student.

My mother used to tell me that when I was in my pram she walked everywhere with me—no hopping into a car for her. Today we're always in such a rush, it sometimes seems like we've lost the art of walking. Here are some prayers to inspire us while we walk, and to make our time fruitful spiritually as well as physically.

Prayer on setting out

But I trust in you, O Lord; I say, 'You are my God.'
PSALM 31:14 (NIV)

Lord, I thank you that you have given me legs to walk and senses to experience what is around me. Whatever my reasons for walking today, please let me commit the time into your hands and be open to what you have to teach me.

Pushing the pram

'Let the little children come to me, and do not hinder them, for the kingdom of God belongs to such as these.'
MARK 10:14B

Lord, thank you for this precious gift of a child. Thank you for all I see around me as I walk. I pray for my child and their future walk

with you. I pray for children everywhere, particularly those who are
in need.

First steps

Then Peter said, 'Silver or gold I do
not have, but what I have I give you. In
the name of Jesus Christ of Nazareth,
walk.'... He jumped to his feet and
began to walk.

ACTS 3:6, 8

The process of learning to walk is
a bit slower for us, Lord! But it's
something most of us can do. And
we can all help people to walk,
whether it's encouraging a child
in their first steps or supporting
someone back to health after illness
or through disability. Lord, thank
you for the privilege of being able
to walk alongside people
in so many ways.

Walking to school/work

'If I send them home hungry, they will
collapse on the way, because some of
them have come a long distance.'

MARK 8:3

We need to be fit to walk, and
walking makes us fit. Thank you,
Lord, that you provide everything
I need for my life. Thank you for
my school or work. I do this walk
so often, I get blasé about it and
my mind goes off on a hundred
and one tangents. I pray that today
I will not miss anything that you
want me to see. I thank you for my
friends and colleagues. I pray that
you will make me sensitive to their
needs and, where necessary, enable
me to see through hard shells to the
real people underneath.

Walking round the supermarket

'I sent you to reap what you have
not worked for. Others have done the
hard work, and you have reaped the
benefits of their labour.'

JOHN 4:38

I've never really thought of praying
in a shop before, Lord. Help me to

make wise choices in the things I buy. I thank you as I reflect on all the people who have worked so that this food is available for me. As my basket gets heavier, I pray for them and the burdens they might be carrying in their lives.

Walking in difficult circumstances

'Come,' [Jesus] said. Then Peter got down out of the boat, walked on the water and came towards Jesus.
MATTHEW 14:29

Lord, I know you won't call me to walk on water, but sometimes the things you expect me to do seem just as impossible. It's much easier just to stay put. Sometimes I don't even want to stand up in case I rock the boat, never mind step out in faith into the unknown. What obstacles might lie ahead…? Please, help me to trust as Peter did, keep my eyes firmly on you, and walk.

Those who can't walk

[Jesus] told them, 'The harvest is plentiful, but the workers are few. Ask the Lord of the harvest, therefore, to send out workers into his harvest field.'
LUKE 10:2

Lord, sometimes I feel as though I can't do much for you, or anyone else really. Thank you that, whether I can physically walk or not, I am still your child and you love me and call me to serve you. Please show me what you want me to do for you today.

Walking in company

Afterwards Jesus appeared in a different form to two of them while they were walking in the country.
MARK 16:12

Thank you, Lord, for the joy of sharing walks with others. Walking is a great time to share feelings. Sometimes it's a bit too easy to get engrossed in the conversation and not see very obvious things on the road. Lord, as I walk through my life, I pray that I may always see with *your eyes. I give you thanks for my companions along the way and pray that I will always be willing to walk with them.*

Walking alone

The Lord God said, 'It is not good for the man to be alone. I will make a helper suitable for him.'
GENESIS 2:18

Lord, although your word tells us that it isn't good to be alone, there are many reasons why we might be. Sometimes the boot is on the other foot and we actually long to be away from the busy throng and may even feel less alone on our own. Lord, whether it's our time to walk alone or our time to be with others, we pray that we will do it resting in your strength and knowing your peace.

Walking the dog

Bring out every kind of living creature that is with you.
GENESIS 8:17A

There's something very steadying and calming about walking a dog. Lord, I thank you for this animal, which gets me out of the house into your creation, whatever the weather, whether I want to or not. Thank you for the people I meet on my travels and for the sense of community I feel with them.

Meditation

I remember a poster I had on my wall as a student. A path leading over a wooden covered-in bridge bearing the sign 'Cross this bridge at a walk'.

Close your eyes and visualise this scene. Imagine Jesus walking alongside you as you cross unhurriedly. Let him point out to you any areas of your life where you need to slow down. Just enjoy being with him.

My Space

This space is for you to make your own notes.

The Pilgrim's Way across to Holy island, or Lindisfarne, off the coast of Northumberland.

article

TONY HORSFALL

Learning to walk

author

Tony Horsfall is a freelance trainer and retreat leader, living in Yorkshire. He has written a number of books, including *Working from a Place of Rest* (BRF, 2010) and *Mentoring for Spiritual Growth* (BRF, 2008) and contributes to *New Daylight* Bible reading notes. For further information, see www.brfonline.org.uk.

In the early part of his life, the famous Chinese Christian leader Watchman Nee was learning what it meant to be seated with Christ (Ephesians 2:6). His middle years were given to Christian service and to walking worthily of the gospel (Ephesians 4:1, 17; 5:2, 8, 15).

Throughout the Bible 'walking' is a metaphor for Christian life and conduct. Watchman Nee did not envisage a life of passivity, but of a step-by-step obedience to the will of God. He himself was very active in ministry, and in his book *Sit, Walk, Stand* he taught that the Christian life must be worked out in practical ways, as described in the middle chapters of Ephesians. 'Sitting describes our position with Christ in the heavenlies,' Watchman Nee wrote. 'Walking is the practical out-working of that heavenly position here on earth. Unless we bring heavenliness into our dwellings and offices, our shops and kitchens, and practise it there, it will be without meaning.'

The great vision that fired his own heart was for the gospel to reach the whole of China. He taught much about the inner life but was always concerned with evangelism, and travelled extensively throughout the country to preach the good news.

Nee quickly saw the potential of literature to reach this goal, and moved to Shanghai in 1927 to begin a publishing ministry, producing a teaching magazine, along with booklets and tracts based on his preaching. These proved to be both popular and effective in spreading the Christian message because his style was simple and uncomplicated. The only book he actually authored—*The Spiritual Man*—was published at this time. The many other books that bear his name were later transcriptions of his spoken messages.

Nee longed to see a local church operating on the principles of the New Testament, and in Shanghai he met others with the same desire. They began meeting together in a 'house' fellowship, free of the trappings of more organised religion. They rejected the need for ordained clergy, concentrating instead on developing the gifts of lay people. They provided their own training conferences for emerging leaders, and attracted many able men to their ranks, so that the movement (nicknamed

The great vision that fired his own heart was for the gospel to reach the whole of China

'The Little Flock') grew quickly. They wanted to see an indigenous Chinese expression of Christianity distinct from that associated with the colonial powers.

The fact that none of the leaders were paid, and that believers were willing to use their homes as meeting places, meant that the movement could expand easily into other parts of the country. As people were transferred in their jobs, new centres for witness were opened up. Some moved voluntarily, taking jobs that allowed them to be involved in ministry as well (many chose to be barbers!) Soon there were more than 200 such workers.

Nee was an enthusiastic leader, influencing many others, but he was not always in good health. He contracted tuberculosis (TB) and had to step back to convalesce, having almost died. Although he recovered, he continued to suffer bouts of the disease. Occasionally too he was afflicted with depression, especially when he found himself the subject of hostile criticism from fellow believers. All of this meant that he rejected extreme forms of the victorious life teaching, reminding his followers that even the apostle Paul 'despaired even of life', and that 'we have this treasure in jars of clay' (2 Corinthians 1:8, 4:7, NIV). Nee often said, 'To keep

> 'To keep our hand on the plough while wiping away our tears—that is Christianity'

our hand on the plough while wiping away our tears—that is Christianity.'

As his ministry grew, and his writings circulated, so his reputation increased. He came into contact with some of the leaders of the Brethren assemblies in London, and visited England in 1933 at their request. While they had much in common, Nee was too 'open' in his fellowship with other Christians and the links petered out. He returned to Britain again in 1938 to speak at the Keswick Convention, and then to travel in Western Europe. His eloquent ministry and gracious manner endeared him to many.

Nee was never satisfied with his experience of God and hungered for more. He was conscious, for example, that he often fought a battle with his temper. He experienced personal renewal through the realisation that everything we need is found in Christ 'who has become for us wisdom from God—that is, our righteousness, holiness and redemption' (1 Corinthians 1:30). The theme of brokenness as a precursor to divine blessing became prominent in his teaching, and while he was open to the emphasis on revival and the work of the Spirit, he felt that some revival methods worked like spiritual opium—addiction to them required an ever-increased dosage.

In early 1942 Nee stepped aside from his ministry to join his brother in establishing a pharmaceutical company. Ostensibly this was to help finance more workers, but his fellow leaders were aghast and withdrew fellowship from him. Rumours circulated as to why Nee took this course of action but there was no evidence of any wrongdoing on his part. Later he admitted to a certain 'boredom' in ministry, perhaps what medieval theologians called the sin of 'accidie' or spiritual sluggishness. Whatever the cause, it took him some time to recover, but in 1948 he made a full confession over his failings and was restored to fellowship in the Little Flock.

He returned to ministry wiser and stronger, and with an increased output in his writings. Perhaps, through the

> Through the trial, God had been preparing him for an even greater challenge

trial, God had been preparing him for an even greater challenge that awaited him when the Communist Party began to gain power in China in 1949. Having learned to walk in the way of Christ, he would soon be called to learn to stand his ground against those who wanted to eliminate Christianity altogether, and who would threaten his very life.

For Reflection

How does Watchman Nee's life help you understand the metaphor of 'walking' as a picture of the Christian life?

Consider prayerfully his watchword: 'To keep our hand on the plough while wiping away our tears—that is Christianity.'

What does Nee's experience of failure and recovery say to you in your own walk with God?

article

HEATHER FENTON

Thinking about ways of walking

Body language can tell us a lot about how someone is feeling. We walk in different ways at different times and, because we are whole people, what is happening on the inside is reflected in the way we walk. There are lots of different ways of walking and how we do so can communicate our feelings

author

Heather Fenton has spent a number of years in parish ministry as well as working as an editor.

to others too. Some of these are listed below, but you may be able to think of some more!

I started to think about this because I remembered walking in a silly, light-hearted way one day towards a friend of mine who had come to visit me. Liz, who is a primary school teacher, asked me why I was 'waving my arms outstretched in the air like an aeroplane'. So without thinking I replied, 'Because it is easier than being a helicopter!' She just stood and laughed! Somehow there I was, back in primary school; it was a fun walk like that and, although it was a while back, I still remember her visit because it started off with this conversation.

So here are some probably more serious ways of walking for your consideration:

* *Reluctantly*—a tired child who is saying, 'Do we have to do this?'
* *Sadly*—'last time I was there I was with…'
* *Dutifully*—'I must take the dog for a walk'
* *Overextended*—the walk that is too long
* *Now impossible*—the sort of thing we used to do but can no longer manage

> What is happening on the inside is reflected in the way we walk

* *Quitting*—walking away unhappily
* *Accidental*—walking into something
* *Quietly tiptoeing*—watching wildlife; sneaking up on someone
* *Walking fast*—trying not to run; urgent or late
* *Extra slowly*—walking with an older person; listening at the same time
* *Tired*—dragging your feet, walking into things
* *Walking with intent*—walking somewhere in order to…
* *Carefully*—walking in the dark
* *Observational walking*—taking time to look around at the detail
* *Walking without noticing*—an accident waiting to happen?
* *Noisy walking*—protesting, stamping, shouting

What have I learnt about myself?

Why not spend some quiet time thinking about these questions? Consider the list of ways of walking we have noticed above. Then ask yourself these questions:

❖ *Walking for work*—following the lawnmower or the vacuum cleaner, for example
❖ *Light-hearted walking, for fun*— pretending to be an animal or a bird to amuse someone else
❖ And yes, even *like a child*—full of energy, bouncing along with a sense of expectation

What have I learnt about myself? What is God saying to me through these things? How is my walk with him reflected in these ways of walking? In what ways would I like to walk with him better? How would I like my walk with him to be? Do I need to walk alongside others in a different sort of way?

Turn your thoughts into prayer.

I remembered walking in a silly, light-hearted way one day towards a friend of mine

Take time to consider:

❖ What sort of walking have I already done today?
❖ What sort suits my mood now?
❖ Which of the above do I do most regularly?
❖ What people or circumstances make me want to do one or more of the above and why?
❖ What is too much for me?
❖ What delights me?

Lord, thinking about it, I know that there are so many ways of walking. All in their time express our feelings as human beings. So I bring to you the hard things I have thought about... I also bring the ways in which I desire to walk to you, especially... I pray for the people who help me to achieve that for which I want to aim... as well as those who always seem to make my walk more difficult...

And most of all, Lord Jesus, I ask that you will help me to walk with you in all the circumstances of my life.

Margaret's Space

Margaret Harvey is a retired priest in the Church in Wales. She has been running Coleg y Groes Retreat House. Margaret writes a regular column in *Quiet Spaces*.

Heather has written about different types of walking. Here are three more ways to add to her list. Each of them has something to tell us about our walk with God. Together they could form an outline for a Quiet Day, especially one that included some walking time.

We live in wonderful walking country here in North Wales, with mountains and wooded valleys to explore, whether you are a serious walker or out for a gentle stroll. On a holiday or a day off we tend to do the sort of walking that is simply for enjoyment. It is a wonderful way to de-stress while losing some weight into the bargain! It is also a very good way into attentive prayer. The rhythm of walking, of putting one foot in front of the other, is stilling in itself. It can be linked with a mantra type of prayer that helps to still and focus the mind. Try walking to the rhythm of the Jesus Prayer: 'Lord Jesus Christ, Son of God, have mercy on

> ... the sort of walking that is simply for enjoyment

The rhythm
of walking

me, a sinner.' Or use a short phrase from scripture or just the name, Jesus. This kind of walking also gives us time to notice what is around us. The Psalms are full of this kind of noticing, which moves naturally into praise.

Psalm 104 is an obvious example and a good psalm to read before setting out on a walk. But many other psalms reveal the writer as someone who notices and relishes details, from nesting birds (Psalm 84:3) to the joyful movement and sound of ripe wheat fields in the breeze (65:13). The psalmist has wide open eyes that don't notice only the lovely and reassuring; for example, he sees the effects of drought (32:4) and reflects on his own spiritual dryness. Our country walk may well include evidence of fly-tipping or thoughtless destruction and lead us into prayer for the society of

> This kind of walking also gives us time to notice what is around us

As we get on with our Christian 'walk', we need the encouragement of looking to the horizon and not always down at our feet

which we are part. Farm machinery or towering windmills on the horizon may encourage us to pray for the economic life of the nation.

The second type of walking has a destination in view. We may walk to school or to work, to the shops or to the station. In the past, in rural areas children walked long distances to school each day and drovers walked with their animals to markets hundreds of miles away. An elderly friend told of how his father, as a boy, used to walk the pigs from the village farms to market 20 miles away, beginning just

after midnight on a Monday morning (so avoiding Sunday). Pigs are not the easiest animals to persuade to move together in an orderly fashion! He must have been very glad to see the market town increasingly clearly as he drew nearer. As we get on with our Christian 'walk', we need the encouragement of looking to the horizon and not always down at our feet. Again and again in the Psalms the writer fixes his sights on God, who is a place to run to (18:2), a light to guide (v. 28), an ultimate hope (27:13–14).

You may be doing a different sort of walking too. When I pass the small gym on the outskirts of our village, I see people on exercise machines, walking away, but never actually moving from the spot. 'Wait for the Lord,' the psalmist writes again and again (for example, Psalm 27:14; 37:34). 'Waiting' can seem like being stuck in the same place when we long to move on. Waiting for God can be very demanding, a time when faith has to be well and truly 'exercised'. But, as with the people in the gym, the exercise makes us stronger. Verses about waiting are often linked with hope and strength and with God's faithfulness. Psalm 40 is all about the results of patient waiting with God—a good psalm to take to the gym!

Teresa of Avila wrote:

Christ has no body now but yours,
No hands, no feet on earth but yours,
Yours are the eyes through which he looks
Compassion on this world,
Yours are the feet with which he walks to
*   do good,*
Yours are the hands with which he blesses
*   all the world.*
Yours are the hands, yours are the feet,
Yours are the eyes, you are his body.

Christ has no body now but yours.

Cast your cares on the Lord and
he will sustain you;
he will never let the righteous fall.
But you, O God, will bring
down the wicked into the pit of
corruption;
bloodthirsty and deceitful men
will not live out half their days.
But as for me, I trust in you.
PSALM 55:22–23 (NIV)

HEATHER FENTON

Walking through the Psalms

I think the book of Psalms is just wonderful. I am old enough to have sung psalms to chants in my village church choir when I was a teenager, so I still find that the old words, together with the chants, spring easily into my mind,

author

Heather Fenton has spent a number of years in parish ministry as well as working as an editor.

often when I am least expecting them. Full of human emotion and experience, psalms draw us into the inner world of their writers and surprisingly resonate with our own humanity. So much for considering ourselves to be more sophisticated!

So come with me for a quick walk through some ideas about walking in the Psalms. Starting at the beginning, we can walk straight into Psalm 1:1 and maybe walk into trouble. Walking with sinners, eh? More clues about what this means come in the same verse, where sinners are identified as those who mock and scorn God's law. Do we encounter mocking and scorn? If so, how would we deal with it? One of the weaknesses of much contemporary Christian living could be that it lacks distinctiveness. Yes, we may 'go' to church, but how about our everyday lives? Are we embarrassed about our Christianity in some company—the company of mockers? Psalm 15:2 puts a more positive light on this. In answer to the rhetorical question in verse 1 (NIV), 'Lord, who may dwell in your sanctuary?' the response is, 'He whose walk is blameless and who does what is righteous, speaks the truth from his heart and has no slander on his tongue…' (see verses 2–5). The psalmist ends confidently, 'he who does these things will never be shaken' (v. 6).

Psalm 23 stands out as a psalm regarding walking, and on pages 6–12 in this issue there is a whole article about this psalm. Maybe it is much loved because it reveals a familiar human emotion of feeling one is trapped in a dark valley, a desert or an enclosed place. The path ahead has yet to be trodden by us and we fear or even experience loss, failure, separation, endless darkness. Reading the life of David, we can see how this comes out of his personal journey as he experiences both 'green pastures' and 'tight corners'. One of these tight corners David encounters receives a mention in Psalm 56:1: 'Men hotly pursue me; all day long they press their

attack' and from verse 5 we can see that the attack is not limited to chasing him, but applies to their words too. Verse 5 says, 'All day long they twist my words; they are always plotting to harm me.' If we have not experienced being chased, we may well have had our words twisted to mean something we had not intended. However, Psalm 56 ends with a confident assertion that God will do something about this, 'that I may walk before God in the light of life' (v. 13). Psalm 23, of course, also ends with the comfortingly confident ring, 'Surely goodness and mercy shall follow me all the days of my life, and I will dwell in the house of the Lord for ever' (v. 6).

Psalm 115 contrasts the Lord with the heathen gods of the surrounding nations. These nations cannot see God; they cannot understand or work him out. Instead, they have idols, gods made of 'silver and gold, made by the hands of men' (v. 4). The psalmist pours scorn on these, pointing out that these idols have mouths but cannot speak, have no sense of hearing or smell, hands that cannot feel, feet that cannot walk. In other words, they are utterly ridiculous man-made things and not gods at all! Well, that brings us sharply into the 21st century. How many man-made things does our society have, made by human hands, which we think we absolutely must have, whatever the cost? Is there a point at which the consumer society tips over into the worship of consumerism? So perhaps these heathen gods are not that far from us too and perhaps people cannot understand about God now any more than they did then?

Trouble will come from these gods, who, Psalm 82:5, 'know nothing, they understand nothing'. Their followers 'walk about in darkness' and a consequence is that 'all the foundations of the earth are shaken' (v. 5). In a global world, it suddenly seems much easier to imagine ways in which 'the foundations of the earth' could actually be shaken. Leaders thinking they are gods themselves (v. 6) 'die like mere men' (v. 7).

Freedom is a basic cry of the human heart but many things bind us up. God intents that his people should walk in the freedom only he can give. The author of that long psalm, Psalm 119, knows about this in his everyday experience when he says, 'I will walk about in freedom, for I have sought out your precepts' (v. 45) and says that he will speak of God's statutes 'before kings' (v. 46). Kings represent the place of earthly power, power that could lead to loss of an individual's freedom if not acknowledged, but in spite of this the writer is willing to speak of God's statues. Perhaps the equivalent would be acknowledging God's importance in some secular working environments these days, even in the face of mocking and scorn.

© Joana Croft

It reveals a familiar human emotion of feeling one is trapped in a dark valley, a desert or an enclosed place

Again, the psalms acknowledge the frailty of being in a tight corner. Psalm 138:7 refers to walking through trouble: 'Though I walk in the midst of trouble, you preserve my life.' When we feel vulnerable, there is Psalm 142:3, part of a prayer written by David when he was in a cave and therefore probably hiding from Saul. His experience is that God, in his love, offers protection and salvation.

Walking is part of the ancient idea of pilgrimage and Psalms 120—134 are 'songs of ascent'. These psalms, also known as gradual psalms, or pilgrim songs, may well have been used by the pilgrims going up, or ascending, to Jerusalem at the three festivals of 'Passover', the 'Feast of Weeks' and the 'Feast of Tabernacles' (see Deuteronomy 16:1—17). Join in with the thrill of the person who first uttered Psalm 122: 'I rejoiced with those who said to me, "Let us go the house of the Lord"' (v. 1). He was already excited at the anticipation of going but now 'our feet are standing in your gates, O Jerusalem' (v. 2). We are actually here at last! How amazing! What a thrill! See what a marvellous place this is: 'Jerusalem is built like a

The psalmist ends confidently

city' (v. 3). The journey may have been filled with the excitement of fellow pilgrims travelling together and singing these psalms, but wow, arriving at the destination is just something else!

So the psalmist walks around Jerusalem taking a good look. 'Walk about Zion, go round her, count her towers, consider well her ramparts, view her citadels' (48:12—13). He then exhorts his listeners to remember, so that they may tell the next generation, for 'this God is our God for ever and ever; he will be our guide even to the end' (v. 14)!

God has 'delivered my soul from death, my eyes from tears, my feet from stumbling, that I may walk before the Lord in the land of the living' (116:8—9), is the conclusion the psalmist has reached. There may be dark and dangerous places, the godless may mock, but his experience is that:

The Lord God is a sun and a shield;
The Lord bestows favour and honour;
no good thing does he withhold
from those whose walk is blameless.
O Lord Almighty, blessed is the man
who trusts in you.
PSALM 84:11—12

LUCY MOORE

Labyrinth for Lent—
or any other time

author

Lucy Moore is BRF's Messy Church Team Leader, an international speaker and an Associate Missioner for Fresh Expressions. Her books include *The Gospels Unplugged*, *The Lord's Prayer Unplugged*, *All-Age Worship*, *Messy Church*, *Messy Crafts*, *Sports Fun for Messy Churches* and others. For more information, see www.brfonline.org.uk. This article first appeared on www.barnabasinchurches.org.uk.

On your marks:

This labyrinth was first devised and used on an all-age parish weekend. It is something that, once set up, can be allowed to run on its own, to be visited by individuals or groups at their convenience. The idea is to provide a way of taking time out for a spiritual check-up, using the format of a visit to a health spa. Lent is the time for this sort of self-examination and perhaps you could set aside part of the church or a hall for a weekend for this activity at the beginning of this season of the church year.

Get set:

Setting up the labyrinth will need some time and thought. You will need eleven spaces at which those travelling the journey can stop, reflect and take part in a simple activity. A traditional labyrinth has these spaces on the way to and from the centre of a winding path. You can find out more about labyrinths and their patterns on the internet. However, keep it simple and merely use whatever large space you have. Divide it up into a series of 'rooms', with some partitions if possible (even just chairs) and leave enough space for up to three or four adults and/or children at a time in each area.

In each room there are some objects to be placed (see below) and also some instructions about what to do, including an appropriate Bible verse for reflection. If you have the time and equipment, then recording the words on to MP3 players for individuals to use would be a great idea. The next section introduces the eleven 'rooms' with the objects needed, the instructions and the Bible verses.

Go!

1. Safe space

You are welcome here. This is your space. This is a safe space. A space to remind yourself of who you are and why you're here. A space to wind and unwind; to retreat and to advance; to withdraw and to move out refreshed. A space to be apart from other people and yet to be aware that you are sharing the space with them, that they are walking alongside you; that their journeys touch yours. And it's a time to remember who brought you here, who paid for you to come in, who designed and made

you and who has a plan for your life; someone who wants only the best for you, the very best.

You are invited to walk this labyrinth at your own pace; to race through or to walk slowly. You might go through it just once or return to it a second time. You cannot do it wrong. The way you enjoy it is the right way for you. You are welcome here. This is your space. This is a safe space.

When you're ready, walk on to the first zone. Then read **Matthew 11:28–29**.

> A space to remind yourself of who you are and why you're here

2. The changing room

Pile of heavy bags/cases and a variety of clothes—some tight and some baggy, some ugly—and a cupboard to place them in

Here you are in the changing room. A place to change. This is a place to leave behind you the things that stop you living life to the full. You can pick them up again later. They will be looked after. Is there anything you would like to take off and put down for a while? Anything that's like a heavy suitcase weighing

you down or like a bag that you're ashamed to be carrying? Perhaps you're feeling uncomfortable, as if you're wearing clothes that don't suit you, or that restrict you and cramp your style. Perhaps there are some valuables that are precious to you but which you need to place in safekeeping for a while to allow you to move freely.

Place one or more items into the cupboard to symbolise the things you want to leave behind for a while. Make sure you've left them behind before you move on to the next zone. Read **Hebrews 12:1**.

3. Personal trainer

Card file box, set of filing cards divided into two with healthy habits/unhealthy habits as headings, pencils

Imagine meeting a personal trainer. This is someone who needs to know everything about you in order to discover what you really need to change—someone who is kind, but clinical, detached and non-judgmental, safe. This trainer may ask incredibly searching and intimate questions, but you can't detect even a trace of criticism, just real and active interest. He or she puts your whole lifestyle under review and is most interested in the things that have become habits: your eating habits, your exercise and your rest habits. The trainer wants to know what you watch, read and listen to, even enquire about your thought habits! This trainer seems to be asking about everything, including things you'd prefer nobody knew about at all, either because you're proud of them or because you're ashamed of them.

Which of your habits do you think you would feel most uncomfortable about telling them? Which would you feel delighted to share with them?

Take a review card and fill in your healthy habits and unhealthy habits that you think are most significant. You can use drawings or notes that nobody but you will understand. Look at what

Scarred but complete and whole

you've noted. What would you like to have changed if you came back in a year's time? Circle it. Is there anything in particular you would like to remember? Underline it. Either take the list with you, or place it safely in the filing box. Now move on to the next zone when you are ready. Read **1 Corinthians 9:24–27**.

4. Exercise

A piece of a racetrack on a flat surface, pipe-cleaners

We're all at different stages of our journey. What does this stage of your life feel like to you? If it were a race, what sort of race might your life be like at the moment?

A treadmill, a hard slog, getting nowhere and no way of jumping off? A sprint—using every ounce of energy for a finishing line just ahead of you? A cross-country run—gritted teeth, pacing yourself for the long-term goal, conserving your energy, enjoying the scenery? An uphill slog? An exhilarating but out-of-control plummet downhill? A refreshment stop? A relay race, taking on the baton from the last team member, looking forward to handing it on to the next? Hurdles—just one obstacle after another? A three-legged race tied to someone slower? Or someone faster?

Make a pipe-cleaner figure of yourself on your race and place it on the racetrack. Read **1 Timothy 4:9–10**.

5. Diet

A tray of pieces of chopped fruit, vegetables, bread and sweets

Food and a healthy diet are crucial to allow you to be the person you're meant to be. Try some of the foods here… give your taste buds time to sense them fully. How much do you enjoy them? Keep trying them as you think…

People don't just need food to live on; they need every word that comes from God. God gave Moses and his people bread, meat and water in the wilderness. Daniel and his friends refused the rich diet of royal food, because it compromised what they believed in; they ate only vegetables and they stayed healthily. Jesus turned down the possibility of satisfying his hunger in the desert because magicking up food would have been the easy way out for him. Yet he fed the 5000 in the wilderness with more than they could manage to eat. He became a miracle and offered himself as living water

> We're all at different stages of our journey

poured out, as the bread that gives daily life, as the wine poured out for our forgiveness. These ordinary everyday foods keep not only our bodies going but our whole human selves in every part of us. Are you what you eat? Read **John 4:13–14 and John 6:35**.

6. The jacuzzi

Either have a few foot spas to use or simply comfy chairs to sit on, bubble mixture and wands

Jump into the jacuzzi! There you sit in the lap of luxury, with warm, scented water lapping around you, which starts quietly to churn and bubble until you are gently pummelled and massaged on every side. You can feel each part of your body being soothed and relaxed. You have all the time in the world. You become very conscious of each of your limbs... toes... feet... ankles... shins... knees... thighs... bottom... hips... waist... stomach... chest... neck... face... head... shoulders... arms... wrists... hands... fingers... You are a delicate yet tough machine, a beautifully balanced piece of art, an intelligent, sensitive, marvellous, incredibly detailed organism. Some parts of you have taken a knock or two over the course of your life. Some parts don't work as well as they used to. But what a wonder you are!

A poet marvelled at his own self. As you hear his words, blow some bubbles in this jacuzzi and, as they pop,

> This is a place to leave behind you the things that stop you living life to the full

give thanks for the different parts of your body and the wonderful way they work together. Read **Psalm 139:1–16, 23–24**.

7. The temple

A picture of a 'red' carpet leading up to a temple door, divided into squares to colour in; some crayons

You are a safe space. You are a space where holy things can happen. A space where beauty and mystery dance together. A space so irresistible that the Spirit of God delights in moving in and setting up house. Location, location, location! A space designed for worship. Like the temple on the hill in the city, your life lights up the lives of those around you at work and at school and at home, because of the dynamic energy of the Spirit of God inside you. Your body is a temple, not of getting more stuff, not of scrambling to the top of the tree, not of being the best at everything, but a temple of the Holy Spirit, where God loves to hang out. Like a pearl necklace hidden in the darkness inside a clay pot. Like the CPU of a PC. Like a SIM card in a mobile.

How would you walk into this temple? How would you expect other people to walk in?

Colour in one square of the red carpet… a sign that because of God's Spirit in you, you are someone to treat with respect, and someone who treats themselves with respect. Read **1 Corinthians 6:19 and Ephesians 2:22**.

8. Jesus on the cross

A set of objects, some designed for luxury and some for torture, for example, cotton wool, sharp nails, velvet, thorns, silk, a (safe) plastic knife

Look at these things. Some of these you would pick up carefully so as not to hurt yourself; you would be anxious if you saw a child anywhere near them. Some are designed for softness and luxury, to make you feel good. Some are designed to damage and destroy a body. It's hard to imagine someone choosing to put themselves on the receiving end of things that hurt.

Carefully pick up and feel the different objects here. Read **Isaiah 53:2–9**.

9. Jesus in majesty

Different full-sized pictures of Jesus in majesty with postcard-sized copies to take away

The last time the women saw Jesus' body, as it was wrapped in cloths and placed in a cave, his body had been broken and was useless, ugly and untouchable. But three days later, they saw him again, transformed, renewed, remade—the same but different. Scarred but complete and whole, filled with energy and beauty beyond their wildest dreams. Not just better, but healed and complete, so that through him the world can be healed and completed. Artists have tried to show what this risen Jesus is like: they draw him on a throne or holding a sceptre, a symbol of power and authority.

Here are some examples. Which do you like best? Can you imagine how it would feel to be best friends with this person?

You have all the time in the world

Take a copy of the picture you like best as you journey out of the labyrinth, to remind you of the way Jesus is both ruler of the universe and at home in your life. Read **Philippians 2:5–11**.

10. The team

Lengths of string in different colours and lengths, the start of a web tied on to a cross

As we turn towards the outside world, we begin to think of our life outside the labyrinth. We don't leave Jesus behind us; instead, he comes with us, goes before us, and walks beside us, wherever we go. And he gives us all the amazing resources of his church to support us on our walk with him—the different people local to us and in the church across the UK and across the world to stand by us as brothers and sisters in a great web of relationships, where we are needed and loved and valued.

Tie some pieces of string on to the web as you thank God for members of the church who have supported you, and commit yourself to being a support to other people in this great worldwide family. Read **Colossians 3:15 and Ephesians 4:2–3**.

11. The vision

Small mirrors, a light

Use the mirrors to make the light dance across the walls. Where's the darkest spot to light up? Jesus asks us to join him in stepping out towards a world in need, bringing his light to dark places at home, at school, at work, in the places he can go only through us. He longs for a world full of wholeness and health, full of that deep down 'shalom' peace that comes from being at peace with God himself. As you let the light dance, think about the different people you'll meet today, tomorrow, in the coming week and imagine Jesus' light dancing into their lives, perhaps through something you say or do. Imagine it bringing wholeness and healing and peace. Let the light dance on to you. And as you go out into the world, take away with you the knowledge that although you can't see it, that light of wholeness and healing and peace goes with you wherever you go.

When you're ready, go in the wholeness and healing and peace of Christ. Read **Luke 4:18–19**.

A space where beauty and mystery dance together

Walking through the landscape of Ann Griffiths and her hymns

Ann Griffiths is a very well-known hymn writer in Wales who began to compose her hymns in about 1802. Born in 1776 at a farm called 'Dolwar Fach' and having been christened at Llanfihangel-yng-Ngwynfa Church, she later became a Calvinistic Methodist. She was a Welsh speaker, and so her hymns and letters

A chapel was opened near her home as a memorial to Ann Griffiths are all in Welsh. Her main influence was scripture and her work springs from her knowledge and understanding of the Bible. Ann died, aged 29, in August 1805 and is buried in the churchyard where she was christened. The following Sunday, John Hughes preached at her funeral service, taking as his text, 'For to me, to live is Christ and to die is gain' (Philippians 1:21, NIV). Ruth, her former maid, must have recognised the value of Ann's hymns and recited them to her husband, who was able to write them down. A year later these hymns were published by the Rev Thomas Charles as *Casgliad o Hymnau* (Collection of Hymns).

In 1904 a chapel was opened near her home as a memorial to Ann Griffiths. The building is an interesting and very unusual example of Arts and Crafts architecture applied to a non-conformist chapel.

Several English translations of her hymns have been made and those by the late Professor H.A. Hodges

She was a
Welsh speaker

(1905–76) are noted for their accuracy. The text of her hymns and letters in modern Welsh orthography, edited by Dr E. Wyn James, is to be found at www.anngriffiths.cardiff.ac.uk/hymns.html. Two of the Hodges translations are set out overleaf, by kind permission of the copyright owners. There is also an Ann Griffiths walk, details of which can be found at www.bbc.co.uk/wales/mid/sites/walks/pages/ann_griffiths.shtml. This seven-mile walk winds down the Vyrnwy valley from Pont Llogel at Llwydiarth to Pontrobert (which is about eleven miles west of Welshpool). It links places associated with Ann's life through a landscape which would have been familiar to her.

The Hen Gapel John Hughes/John Hughes Memorial Chapel, in Pontrobert near Meifod, is also connected with Ann.

Her main influence was scripture and her work springs from her knowledge and understanding of the Bible

Next door is the cottage that was home for 40 years to the weaver who married Ruth, who had been Ann's maid and was responsible for saving her hymns for posterity. Information regarding this can be found at www.capeli.org.uk/english/john-hughes.pdf.

> Ruth, her former maid, must have recognised the value of Ann's hymns

IV

1. Wholly counter to my nature
Is the path ordained for me;
Yet I'll tread it, yes, and calmly,
While thy precious face I see;
Count the cross a crown, and bear it,
Cheerful live 'mid all life's woes—
This the Way which, straight though tangled,
To the heavenly city goes.

2. Old it is, yet never ageing,
And its name is Wonderful;
Ne'er begun, yet new for ever,
Making dead men rise up whole;

Winning all who travel by it;
Head and Husband 'tis to me;
Sacred way, I'll pass along it
Till in it my rest shall be.

3. Eye of kite could ne'er discern it,
Though it shines with noontide blaze;
None can tread it, none can see it,
Save where faith its light displays;
Breaking ne'er the law of justice,
Godless souls it justifies,
Leads them to God's peace and favour,
Bids the dead to life arise.

4. Way made straight before creation,
Kept to be revealed at need,
When in days of old, in Eden,
God proclaimed the woman's Seed;
His new covenant's foundation,
Once decreed ere time began,
'Tis the wine whose ample virtue
Glads the heart of God and man.

XXIX

I'll walk on softly day by day,
The cross o'ershadowing all my way,
And as I walk, my course I'll run,
And as I run I'll stand and see
The full salvation that shall be
When I'm no more beneath the sun.

Mary Jones
and her walk to get a Bible

Mary Jones was born in December 1784 into a poor family of weavers. She learned to read in the circulating schools organised by Thomas Charles of Bala, and it became her greatest wish that she should have her own copy of the Bible. The nearest copy was kept at a farm two miles from where she lived, and she thought that Bala was the nearest place she could get one for herself. So in 1800, when she was 15, she set out barefoot on a 26-mile walk across one of the most rugged parts of Snowdonia in North Wales. Her determination must have been great as it had taken her six years to save the 17 shillings she needed to buy a Bible.

According to one version of the story, she was very disappointed when, upon reaching Bala, Mr Charles told her that all of the copies which he had were sold or already spoken for. It is said that she was so distraught that Thomas Charles let her buy one of the copies already promised to someone else. In another version of the story, she had to wait two days for a supply of Bibles to arrive. She was then able to purchase a copy for herself and two other copies for members of her family.

Whichever it was—and the second version of the story sounds less likely as she would not have had enough money—it was the impression that Mary Jones left upon him that inspired Thomas Charles and some colleagues to set up what was to become the British and Foreign Bible Society. So her walk became of considerable importance and not just to her.

If you want to follow Mary Jones' footsteps, there is a Mary Jones Walk that starts at Llanfihangel-y-Pennant. To get there, follow the brown signs for Castell-y-Bere from the centre of Abergynolwyn, off the B4405. You should pass the parking for Castell-y-Bere on your left and continue along the minor road until you reach Llanfihangel-y-Pennant, which is only a small hamlet. There is parking on the right, across the road from the church.

There you will see the Mary Jones monument and the village church she attended with her family. Using this walk, you can follow in her footsteps, past lakes named Tal-y-Llyn and Llyn Cau, in the shadow of Cadair Idris, over narrow stiles and fast-flowing streams before you eventually glimpse the shiny expanse of Bala Lake. At the other end of the lake lies the small town of Bala, where plaques on the wall of Barclays Bank depict the spot where Mary received her Bible.

The Long Distance Walkers Association website has a page for the Mary Jones Walk from Llanfihangel-y-Pennant to Bala at www.ldwa.org.uk/index.php.

You can also find out more, including how you might help to raise funds for Bible Society, by going to www.biblesociety.org.uk/support-us/fundraising/mary-jones-walk.

My Space

This space is for you to make your own notes.

The Pilgrim's Way across to Holy island, or Lindisfarne, off the coast of Northumberland.

© Heather Fenton 2010

Two 'psalms of ascent'

set to traditional Welsh tunes

Psalm 122

Tune: Hiraeth

1. With great joy I heard them call me,
'Come with us to see the Lord's house,'
So at last our feet are standing
In the gates of God's own city.

2. O Jerusalem, a city
Built with harmony and order.

Here the tribes of Israel gather;
Here the King meets with his people.

3. May God's peace be with your people,
May your dwellings know God's safety,
All who dwell within you prosper.
I will pray, 'Peace be upon you.'

©MARGARET HARVEY 2000

❖❖❖

Psalm 124

Tune: Ar hyd y Nos

1. What if God had not been for us,
O Israel.
When our enemies attacked us,
O Israel.
Then they would have overwhelmed us
In their furious rage against us;
Then the torrent would have drowned us,
O Israel.

2. Let us praise the Lord who saves us,
Thanks be to God.
Enemies have not destroyed us,
Thanks be to God.
Like a bird escaped from danger
When the hunter's trap is broken:
Our help comes from God Almighty!
Thanks be to God.

©MARGARET HARVEY 2000

Prayer by Lancelot Andrewes

*Lord Jesus, we give you our hands
to do your work. We give you our
feet to walk in your way. We give
you our tongues to speak your
word. We give you our hearts to
love you, now and for ever. Amen.*

LANCELOT ANDREWES 1555–1626

Prayer

The man of integrity walks securely, but he who takes a crooked path will be found out.

PROVERBS 10:9 (NIV)

Whether you turn to the right or to the left, your ears will hear a voice behind you, saying, 'This is the way; walk in it.'

ISAIAH 30:21 (NIV)

HEATHER FENTON

A quick tour of
the history of
pilgrimage

The idea of a sacred journey is very old. The Bible may be seen as a journey of exile from the garden of Eden (Genesis 2:17) to the destination of the new Jerusalem (Revelation 21:2). Abraham, whose story begins in Genesis 12, can

author

Heather Fenton wrote her dissertation for her Master's Degree on pilgrimage and sacred place.

be seen as an early pilgrim, travelling to an unfamiliar destination in response to the call of God.

Later on, when the people of God become a settled people in the land which God has given them, there is still the possibility of a sacred journey, this time to the temple in Jerusalem. They are given three pilgrim festivals (Exodus 23:14–17; Deuteronomy 16:16) and have psalms of ascent (Psalms 120–134) to use on these occasions. Jesus himself went on one such annual pilgrimage as a child (Luke 2:41–42).

The writer of the letter to the Hebrews sees Christians as strangers and pilgrims (Hebrews 12:22–24), exhorting his readers to 'make level paths for your feet' (v. 13, NIV). After the New Testament era, and when the persecution of Christians ceased, people wanted to see the places connected with the Gospels. One of the first Christian pilgrims was Helena, the mother of the Emperor Constantine I, who visited Jerusalem in the late 320s. The idea soon caught on.

apparently faultless lives, spread to all of the known world.

Trade routes helped to encourage this, and it meant that Middle Eastern ideas came to be adapted here in the far western seaboards of Europe. The Celtic Christian pilgrims, known as 'peregrini', saw travel as a form of outreach, and this era became known as the 'age of the saints' (fifth to eighth centuries).

> ... the possibility of a sacred journey, this time to the temple in Jerusalem

Another new fashion was living in the desert in order to be alone, but all too soon the people who did this became the objects of pilgrimage themselves. Soon ideas about travelling to places directly connected with the Gospels, or with those who lived

As a result of their wanderings, many outposts of the Christian faith, often in the form of monastic settlements, were founded in Western Europe. They also invented the idea of 'virtual pilgrimage'. *The Voyage of Brendan*, an 'Otherworld' voyage, can be seen as a way of

a literary pilgrimage tale

experiencing a pilgrimage without having to leave home.

In the later medieval period what may be described as 'destination' pilgrimage developed considerably. Visiting the shrines of saints to obtain their help and prayers was the focus of most pilgrimages. There was less simplicity, and asceticism gave way to a focus on generating finance at the shrines and, for the pilgrims, on obtaining healing or forgiveness. Some rich people even paid poorer people to go on pilgrimage for them in the hope of gaining the advantages without having to make the effort! Eventually this almost came to an end at the time of the Reformation, although Holywell in North Wales is notable for having survived the revolution, maybe because the income generated there was exceptional.

At the Reformation some pilgrimage places hid their treasures. One of these was Pennant Melangell, in rural Powys, where they hid their shrine. Now restored, it is a pilgrimage centre visited by many people (www.st-melangell.org.uk). In the 17th century, John Bunyan wrote *A Pilgrim's Progress*. Like *The Voyage of Brendan*, this was a literary pilgrimage tale but reflecting a very different era. Literal pilgrimage became fashionable again in mid-Victorian times when the travel agent Thomas Cook led his first party to Jerusalem. By the end of the 19th century, he had taken 12,000 people to visit the Holy Land.

Since then pilgrimage destinations old and new have been visited by many thousands of visitors. Destinations include Santiago de Compostela, Lourdes, Walsingham, Taizé, Iona and Medjugorje. Part of the experience of pilgrimage is vulnerability and separation from all that is familiar. This is harder to achieve given the limited amount of time most people are able to put aside for such journeys. However, pilgrimages can be opportunities to learn, and to pray and walk (literally or metaphorically) together, giving inner space for reflection. Finally, there is the return home, being the same and yet having been changed by the experience.

There are, of course, lots of pilgrimage route but here are some pilgrimage websites you may find useful:

www.northerncross.co.uk
www.scottishcross.org.uk
www.smallpilgrimplaces.org
pilgrim.peterrobins.co.uk/wales
www.pilgrims-way-north-wales.org

DAVID SPRIGGS

Acts
(The People's Bible Commentary)

People's Bible Commentary on Acts. For more information about this and other Bible commentaries in the series, visit www.brfonline.org.uk/commentaries-pbc.

author

The Revd Canon Professor Loveday Alexander is Emeritus Professor of Biblical Studies at the University of Sheffield, Visiting Professor at the University of Chester, and Canon Theologian at Chester Cathedral.

Bilbo often used to say that there was only one Road; that it was like a great river: its springs were at every doorstep, and every path was its tributary. 'It's a dangerous business, Frodo, going out of your door,' he used to say. 'You step into the Road, and if you don't keep your feet, there is no knowing where you might be swept off to.'

J.R.R. TOLKIEN, *THE LORD OF THE RINGS: THE FELLOWSHIP OF THE RING*, ALLEN & UNWIN, 1966, P. 83

Welcome to the journey!

'This book will make a traveller of thee,' says John Bunyan at the beginning of *The Pilgrim's Progress*; and the same could well be said of the Acts of the Apostles. Acts is the story of a journey.

It tells the story of the birth of the Church, and its journey outwards and across the world from where it all began, in an upstairs room in Jerusalem. Woven into this story are the journeys of a whole host of individual travellers, apostles and others, moving back and forth across that Mediterranean world and spreading the word wherever they go. But it's also the story of the journey of faith, a journey to which every reader is invited: it's no accident that one of Luke's favourite metaphors for discipleship is 'the Way'.

As so often in the Bible, the journey starts with a vision, which empowers and controls the travellers and to which they constantly revert. The story begins on a mountain-top, the classic location for vision in the Bible, where the

Acts is the story of a journey

heavens open and angels and mortals speak face to face (ch. 1). Then comes the comAmunal visionary experience of Pentecost, when the empowerment of God's Spirit becomes something visible even to the crowds in a Jerusalem street (ch. 2). Further into the narrative, the two controlling visions are Peter's rooftop trance (ch. 10) and Paul's encounter with the risen Christ on the Damascus road (ch. 9); each is recounted over and over again, as the characters in the story are challenged to unravel the true significance of what God is saying to them (chs. 11; 15; 22; 26). And vision provides not only the starting point for mission but also its content: 'we cannot but speak of the things which we have seen and heard' (4:20; 26:19).

Journey into outer space

Like any road movie, Acts contains a strong geographical element. It's the one book in the New Testament where you really need to keep an eye on the map. Most Bibles include a map of 'The Journeys of St Paul', and there are excellent maps available in Bible atlases and other guides. (Tip: a modern physical map of the eastern Mediterranean will

> The story begins on a mountain-top, the classic location for vision in the Bible

often give you a much better flavour of the terrain covered in the book.) More than any other book of the New Testament, Acts conveys a sense of the excitement and romance of travel. It's a cosmopolitan book, moving with ease from the narrow streets of Jerusalem to the classical elegance of Athens, from the high passes of the Turkish-Syrian border to the back streets of Rome. And on the way we meet a variety of deftly drawn characters, from the Ethiopian court treasurer (ch. 8) to the friendly Roman centurion Julius (ch. 27). Acts reminds us that there's a big wide world out there—a daunting prospect to the Galilean disciples on the Mount of

> The characters in the story are challenged to unravel the true significance of what God is saying to them

> It's the one book in the
> New Testament where you
> really need to keep an eye
> on the map

Olives, as Jesus gives them their marching orders (1:8). But gradually, as we read, we come to share with them the unfolding excitement of finding that God is out there too, waiting to meet them and surprise them in this strange world that is also God's world.

Journey into inner space

There's also a more hidden journey, a journey of discovery in which the familiar turns out to be more surprising than we thought. 'Who will show me the way?' asks the Ethiopian, sitting in his chariot on the Gaza road and poring over an ancient scroll (8:31). It's not a road map he's asking for but a new way to read the age-old scriptures, and that's what Philip provides (8:35). Acts conducts its characters (and therefore its readers) into an inner journey of exploration under the guidance of God's Holy Spirit, working out how the 'this' of personal experience corresponds with

the 'that' of God's revelation. This is not always an easy thing to do. Often it means facing up to the puzzlement and hostility of our closest compatriots. Even harder, it means confronting our own prejudices and facing up to our own persistent refusal to recognise God's Spirit at work. So there's a lot of conflict built into the story of Acts; and some of the shortest journeys in the book, geographically speaking, turn out to be some of the longest and most significant in terms of inner space.

A guide for time travellers

This commentary is designed as a kind of interactive travel guide for readers of Acts, helping you to relate to Luke's story on three levels. My first priority is to describe the journey itself from the point of view of the author and his first readers, taking pains to listen carefully

> Acts conveys a
> sense of the
> excitement and
> romance of travel

to the story as he tells it, to pick up the clues he has laid for informed readers, and to try first of all to understand the story in its own terms. This is a basic courtesy we owe to any book, especially to a book written 2000 years ago in a very different culture from our own. That means trying to experience the journey from the viewpoint of the characters in Luke's story, hearing the conversations and debates from inside, trying to understand both sides before jumping to conclusions about what's going on. It also means trying to hear Luke's story through the ears of his original readers, asking about the literary echoes or political resonances that would be picked up by a first-century audience.

Secondly, we can take a step back and ask how Luke's story relates to other stories we know of from that time and place. This means filling in some of the historical information we need, to understand the significance of Luke's story: who was this emperor or that official? What else was going on at the time? How does Luke's version of events tie in with other evidence—Paul's letters, for example? I have tried to indicate

> ... a new way to read the age-old scriptures

what the main historical questions are and where you can find out more if you want to.

And thirdly, we need to move back into the 21st century (which of course we never really left) and ask how Luke's story relates to our own stories. There are many different kinds of travel guides, but most of them fall into two categories: those that offer an armchair substitute for travel, and those that incite you to get out there and sample the real thing. My hope and prayer is that readers will find this guide provoking in many different ways, and that you will be able to use it to inform and inspire your own journeying on the Way, whether individually or as a group. So each reading ends with a question, a quotation or a prayer, suggesting ways to link up with some of the stories that belong to our lives today—things that are happening in the newspapers, or in our churches, or in our own spiritual lives. Use these any way you want, and treat them as a springboard to make your own connections between Luke's world and ours—or simply as a framework for your own prayers.

Quiet Spaces subscriptions

Quiet Spaces is published three times a year, in May, September and January. To take out a subscription, please complete this form, indicating the month in which you would like your subscription to begin.

❑ I would like to take out a subscription myself

Name _____

Address _____

Postcode _____ Telephone Number _____

Email _____

❑ Please do not send me further information about BRF publications.

❑ I would like to give a gift subscription (please complete your name and address above and details of the person you want to give a subscription to below)

Gift subscription name _____

Gift subscription address _____

_____

_____ Postcode _____

Please send beginning with the May 12 / Sep 12 / Jan 13 issue: (delete as applicable)

(please tick box)   UK   SURFACE   AIRMAIL

Quiet Spaces   ❑ £16.95   ❑ £19.05   ❑ £21.60

Please complete the payment details below and send this coupon, with payment to: BRF, 15 The Chambers, Vineyard, Abingdon OX14 3FE.

Method: ❑ Cheque (payable to BRF) ❑ Mastercard ❑ Visa ❑ Maestro

Card no. ❑❑❑❑❑❑❑❑❑❑❑❑❑❑❑❑❑❑

Valid from ❑❑❑❑ Expires ❑❑❑❑ Issue no. of Maestro card ❑❑❑

Security Code ❑❑❑

Signature _____ Date ____ / ____ / ____

All orders must be accompanied by the appropriate payment.

BRF is a Registered Charity   PROMO REF: QSWALK

To order *Quiet Spaces* or other BRF publications mentioned in this journal, visit your local Christian bookshop or go to BRF's website www.brfonline.org.uk.

![brf logo]

Quiet Spaces

The brf prayer and spirituality journal

Walk

Travelling companions

Holy wandering

The path lit by Christ

ISSUE 22

MAY 2012

Prayer and Spirituality Resources

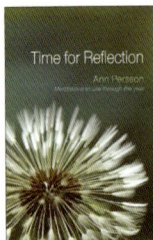

Time for Reflection

Ann Persson

Ann Persson provides practical exercises of varying lengths for exploring contemplative, creative prayer. The themes are linked to relevant Bible passages as well as the Christian calendar and the seasons of nature. A helpful resource for small groups as well as individual use.

pb, 978 1 84101 876 8, £8.99

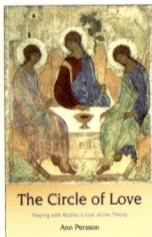

The Circle of Love

Ann Persson

Beginning with her own experience of gazing at the icon during convalescence from surgery, Ann Persson shares her journey of discovery through some of the historic and artistic traditions of icon-painting. She provides a detailed commentary on the image itself and also reflects on the Bible story that inspired the icon.

pb, 978 1 84101 750 1, £5.99

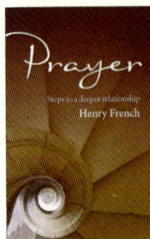

Prayer

Henry French

An introduction to going deeper in prayer, ranging from contemplation to 'prayer on the run'. Each chapter is interspersed with practical exercises to 'earth' the point in hand. Concludes with a section of questions for reflection and personal application.

pb, 978 1 84101 861 4, £6.99

Simple Gifts

Kevin Scully

We are familiar with the idea of friendship or hospitality as gifts. We may dislike other aspects of life, such as ignorance, grief and anger. Drawing on scripture, song, poetry and insights from daily life, Kevin Scully considers ten such gifts. He shows how each can be a source of personal wonder and joy and can draw us closer to God and to one another.

pb, 978 1 84101 851 5, £ 7.99

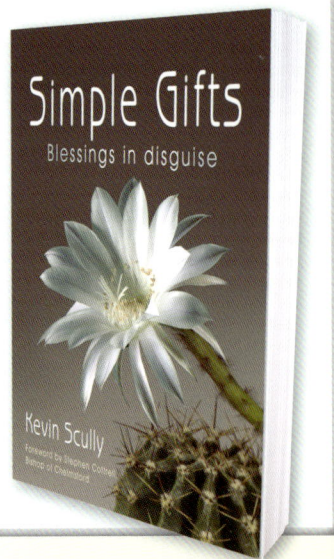

Available from your local Christian bookshop or, in case of difficulty, from BRF **www.brfonline.org.uk** 01865 319700